COOL

STRUCTURES

CREATIVE ACTIVITIES THAT MAKE MATH & SCIENCE
FUN FOR KIDS!

ANDERS HANSON

A Division of ABDO
ABDO
Publishing Company

AND ELISSA MANN

VISIT US AT WWW.ABDOPUBLISHING.COM

Published by ABDO Publishing Company, a division of ABDO, P.O. Box 398166, Minneapolis, Minnesota 55439. Copyright ® 2014 by Abdo Consulting Group, Inc. International copyrights reserved in all countries. No part of this book may be reproduced in any form without written permission from the publisher. Checkerboard Library™ is a trademark and logo of ABDO Publishing Company.

Printed in the United States of America, North Mankato, Minnesota
062013
112013

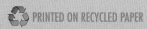 PRINTED ON RECYCLED PAPER

Design and Production: Anders Hanson, Mighty Media, Inc.
Series Editor: Liz Salzmann
Photo Credits: Anders Hanson, Shutterstock

LIBRARY OF CONGRESS CATALOGING-IN-PUBLICATION DATA

Hanson, Anders, 1980-
Cool structures : creative activities that make math & science fun for kids! / Anders Hanson and Elissa Mann.
    pages cm. -- (Cool art with math & science)
Includes index.
ISBN 978-1-61783-825-5
1. Building--Juvenile literature. 2. Architecture--Juvenile literature. 3. Geometry--Juvenile literature.
4. Mathematical recreations--Juvenile literature. 5. Scientific recreations--Juvenile literature.
6. Creative activities and seat work--Juvenile literature. I. Mann, Elissa, 1990- II. Title.
TH149.H36 2013
507.8--dc23
                    2013001900

CONTENTS

COOL STRUCTURES

BITS AND PIECES PUT TOGETHER

Structures are useful arrangements of materials. They have many different parts and pieces. The pieces come together to give the structure form and function. Structures provide shelter, transportation, and **culture**. Some of the most popular **destinations** in the world are structures. The Statue of Liberty, the Eiffel Tower, the Golden Gate Bridge, and the Egyptian pyramids are a few examples of world famous structures.

Skyscrapers tower over many cities. Burj Khalifa in Dubai is the tallest structure in the world. It is 2,717 feet (828 m) tall!

Bridges help people cross gaps. The Golden Gate Bridge is one of the most famous bridges in the world!

PYRAMIDS
ANCIENT GEOMETRY

Thousands of years ago, the Egyptians built pyramids out of stone. They were the first great structures. The largest Egyptian pyramid is the Great Pyramid of Giza. It is the oldest of the Seven Wonders of the Ancient World. It is the only one still standing today. It was the tallest building in the world for more than 3,800 years!

The Egyptian pyramids aren't just amazing buildings. They are also geometric forms. A pyramid is a 3-D shape with triangular sides. The sides meet at a point called the apex. The base of a pyramid can be any type of polygon. The ancient pyramids in Egypt have square bases. They are called square pyramids.

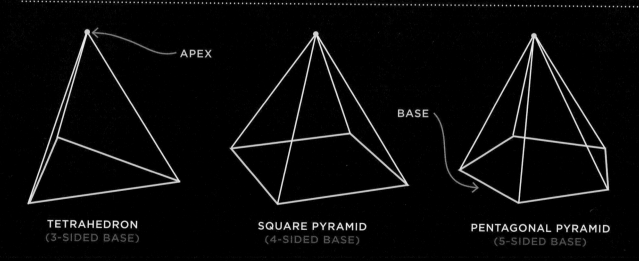

TYPES OF PYRAMIDS

APEX

BASE

TETRAHEDRON
(3-SIDED BASE)

SQUARE PYRAMID
(4-SIDED BASE)

PENTAGONAL PYRAMID
(5-SIDED BASE)

PROJECT

1

BUILD A PYRAMID

◆◆◆◆◆◆◆◆

STUFF YOU'LL NEED

- 30/60/90 TRIANGLE
- A LARGE PIECE OF CARDBOARD
- PENCIL
- SCISSORS
- DUCT TAPE
- FOAM BRUSH
- MOD PODGE
- SAND

TERMS

- ANGLE
- DEGREE
- PYRAMID
- SQUARE
- PENTAGONAL
- TETRAHEDRON
- TRIANGLE

Follow in the footsteps of the ancient Egyptians. Make your own square pyramid! But don't stop there. Make a tetrahedron too, using four triangles. Or try a pentagonal pyramid using one more triangle. Before you know it, you'll have a city of pyramids!

Tip: A 30/60/90 triangle is a type of triangle **template**. You can find them at most art supply stores.

HOW TO MAKE IT

1   Use a 30/60/90 triangle to draw a 60-degree angle on the cardboard. Make the lines as long as you want. The longer the lines, the bigger your pyramid will be.

2   Flip the 30/60/90 triangle over. Line the bottom of the triangle up with the bottom line you just drew. Draw a line that connects the two lines you drew in step 1.

3   Carefully cut out the triangle. Trace around the triangle on the cardboard.

4 Trace two more triangles on the cardboard. Cut out the triangles.

5 Lay the four cardboard triangles next to each other with their sides lined up. Tape the triangles together. Put tape on the side of one of the end triangles.

6 Fold the taped triangles up so the tape is on the inside. Line up the sides of the end triangles. Use the tape to hold them together. The triangles are the sides of your square pyramid.

7 Use a foam brush to spread Mod Podge on one of the sides. Sprinkle a lot of sand over the Mod Podge.

8 Repeat step seven for the other three sides. Let the Mod Podge dry completely.

BRIDGES
GET OVER IT!

S ince the dawn of history people have built bridges. Bridges **span** obstacles. They help people cross from one place to another. The first bridges were simple. They were made of rope, stone, or logs. Today's bridges are more **complex**. They use many different materials and designs.

THE MIGHTY TRIANGLE

The triangle is the strongest polygon. It is very hard to bend or break. Because of their strength, triangles are often used in bridges.

BEAM BRIDGE

A beam bridge is the simplest bridge. It lies in a straight line, going from one side to another.

ARCH BRIDGE

An arch bridge rises in the middle. The arch is held up on each end by supports called abutments.

SUSPENSION BRIDGE

Strong cables support suspension bridges. The cables are attached to big towers. The cables are held down at each end of the bridge by heavy blocks.

14

PROJECT

2

BUILD A BRIDGE

◆ ◆ ◆ ◆ ◆ ◆ ◆

A good bridge can support a lot of weight. Bridge builders often use triangles to construct strong bridges. Try building your own triangle bridge. Using a lot of triangles will help make your bridge strong!

STUFF YOU'LL NEED

- QUICK GRIP GLUE OR ANOTHER ALL-PURPOSE PERMANENT ADHESIVE
- NEWSPAPER
- 43 ½-INCH-WIDE WOODEN CRAFT STICKS
- BINDER CLIPS

TERMS

- DIAGONALLY
- TRIANGLE
- PARALLEL

HOW TO MAKE IT

1 Glue four craft sticks together, end-to-end. Let the glue dry. Glue three craft sticks together, end-to-end. Let the glue dry.

2 Use two craft sticks to connect the rods you made in step 1. Glue each end of a craft stick to one end of each rod. Glue each end of the second craft stick to the other ends of the rods. Let the glue dry.

3 Arrange six craft sticks across the frame you made in step 2. The craft sticks should form equal-sized triangles inside the frame.

4 Glue the six craft sticks to the frame. Use binder clips to hold the sticks in place.

5 Repeat steps 1 to 4 to make a second frame. Let the glue on both frames dry. Remove the binder clips from the frames.

6 Have a friend hold the frames parallel to each other. The longer rods should be on the bottom. Glue craft sticks diagonally across the shorter rods. Glue some of them above and some below the top rods.

7 Turn the bridge over and glue craft sticks diagonally across the longer rods. Use the same process as step 6.

8 Turn the bridge back over. Glue more craft sticks across the bottom rods. Arrange them so they cover the space between the frames.

9 Test the weight your bridge can hold! Balance the bridge between two chairs. Add weight to the middle of the bridge. See how much it will hold.

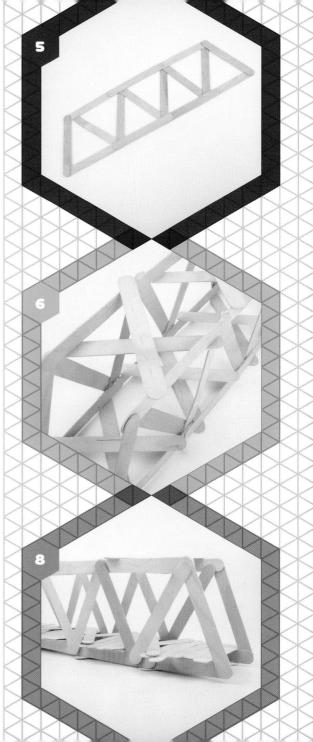

SLING IT!
STRUCTURES IN ACTION!

Catapults and slingshots are simple but effective machines. To build one, you need something stretchy, such as a rubber band. You can stretch or twist a rubber band but it returns to its original shape when you let go.

POTENTIAL ENERGY

Some materials have potential energy. Potential energy is stored energy. It's ready to spring into action at any time. Stretching a rubber band charges it with potential energy. When the rubber band is released, it moves! That's called kinetic energy.

POTENTIAL ENERGY

Pulling on the bands stretches them. They become charged with potential energy.

KINETIC ENERGY

Kinetic energy is action! All moving objects have kinetic energy. It keeps objects in motion. Shooting an object from a **slingshot flings** it through the air. The more kinetic energy it has, the farther it will go!

CONSERVATION OF ENERGY

Energy cannot be created or destroyed. It can only be changed into a different type of energy. The potential energy in a stretched rubber band equals the kinetic energy of the object it shoots. In other words, the more you pull back, the farther it will fly!

KINETIC ENERGY

Releasing the bands turns the potential energy into kinetic energy. The bands snap forward and the ball goes flying!

PROJECT

3

BUILD A CATAPULT

STUFF YOU'LL NEED

- 22 ½-INCH-WIDE WOODEN CRAFT STICKS
- 16 REGULAR RUBBER BANDS
- QUICK GRIP GLUE OR ANOTHER ALL-PURPOSE PERMANENT ADHESIVE
- PLASTIC SPOON
- A SMALL, SOFT OBJECT
- BINDER CLIPS (OPTIONAL)

TERMS

- PARALLEL
- TRIANGLE
- SQUARE

Catapults are ancient structures used to launch heavy objects. They were popular in the **Middle Ages**. When the cannon was invented, the catapult fell out of use. Make a catapult of your own with craft sticks and rubber bands.

Tip: Use binder clips to hold the craft sticks together while the glue is drying.

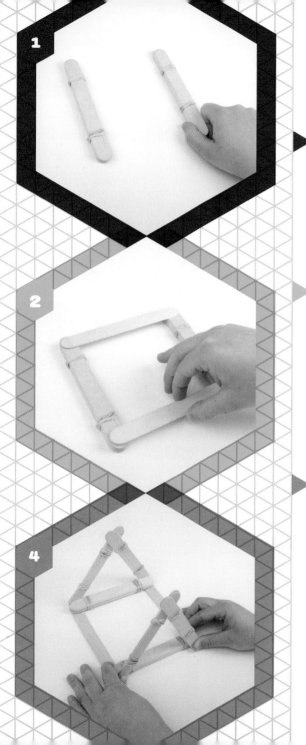

HOW TO MAKE IT

1   Lay six craft sticks on top of each other. Wind a rubber band tightly around each end of the **stack**. Make a second stack of six craft sticks the same way. Lay the stacks parallel to each other.

2   Glue a craft stick across the stacks at each end to make a square base. Let the glue dry.

3   Stack two craft sticks. Wind a rubber band tightly around each end. Make three more stacks of two craft sticks the same way.

4   Hold two of the stacks upright. **Overlap** the tops to form a triangular shape. Glue the tops to each other. Glue the bottoms to one side of the base. Glue the other two stacks to the other side of the base the same way.

5 Attach the handle of the spoon to the middle of a craft stick. Use a rubber band to tie them together tightly.

6 Pull up a loop from one of the rubber bands on the base. Twist the loop. Put one end of the stick with the spoon through the loop. Repeat on the other side. You should be able to move the spoon up and down.

7 Wrap a rubber band around the tops of the triangles.

8 Raise the spoon and put it inside the rubber band that goes across the top of the **catapult**.

9 Pull the spoon down and load it with a small, soft object. Release the spoon and watch the object fly!

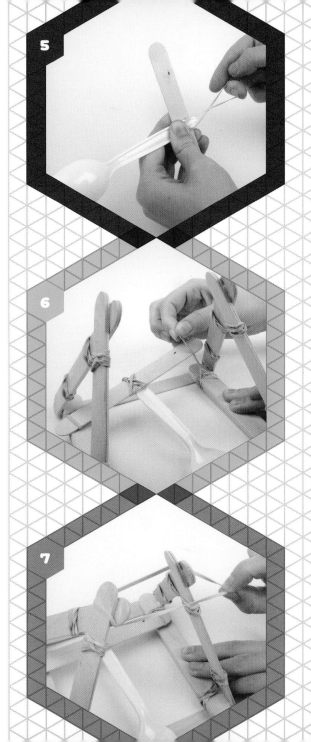

TOWERS
BUILDING HIGH

With the right materials and geometry, buildings can reach the sky! There are two important rules for building tall towers. First, a tall, skinny building can fall over easily. Adding a wide base makes it more stable. Second, towers can **buckle** under their own weight. Using strong, stiff shapes, such as triangles, keeps a tower from breaking.

BRACED RECTANGLE

A braced rectangle has two diagonal beams across it. They support the sides of the rectangle. This makes the rectangle much stronger.

Three braced rectangles can form a triangular prism.

BRACED RECTANGLE

TRIANGULAR PRISM

BRACED RECTANGLES ON THE EIFFEL TOWER

Using the right geometry when designing and building tall buildings is important. Two types of geometry are often used. These are braced rectangles and trusses. Most tall buildings use one or both of these types of geometry.

TRUSS

Trusses are made of many equilateral triangles. The triangles help spread out the load.

Several trusses can be combined to create a space frame.

TRUSS

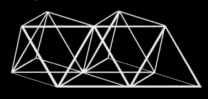

SPACE FRAME

TRUSSES ON AN ELECTRICAL TOWER

26

PROJECT

4

SPAGHETTI TOWER CHALLENGE

◆ ◆ ◆ ◆ ◆ ◆ ◆

▶ **STUFF YOU'LL NEED**

- SPAGHETTI NOODLES
- MARSHMALLOWS
- TENNIS BALL
- RULER

TERMS

- HEIGHT
- LENGTH
- PYRAMID
- FACE
- TRIANGLE
- PRISM

Build a tower using only spaghetti and marshmallows! How high can you make it? Can the top of the tower support a tennis ball? Make sure the tower won't fall over when you add the tennis ball.

This project doesn't include specific building instructions. Instead, it shows how to make some useful parts. It's up to you to connect them. Think creatively and try different models.

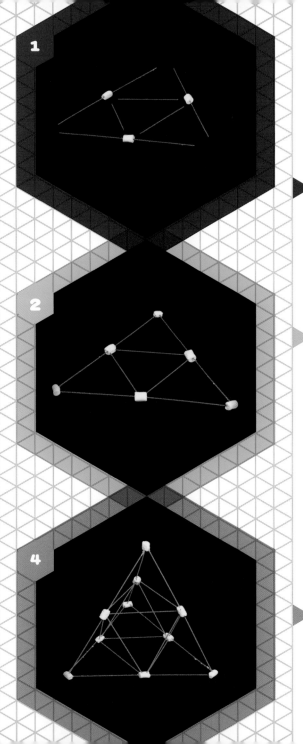

HOW TO MAKE
A PYRAMID BASE

Pyramids work well at the base of a tower. They spread out the weight of the tower.

1 Arrange three long sticks of spaghetti in a triangle. Slide a marshmallow to the middle of each one. Make three sticks half the length of the long sticks. Arrange the short sticks in a triangle inside the long sticks.

2 Connect the ends of the long sticks with marshmallows. Connect the short sticks to the middle marshmallows. This is the base of the pyramid.

3 Slide marshmallows halfway down three more long sticks. Put one end of each stick into the marshmallow at a point of the large triangle. Bring the other ends together. **Insert** them into a single marshmallow.

4 Make nine more half-size sticks. Use the short sticks to connect the middle marshmallows of the long sticks. Use three on each face.

HOW TO MAKE A PRISM TOWER

Prisms work well at the top of a tower. They're great for making tall structures. But they don't offer as much support as **pyramids**.

1 Push two long sticks of spaghetti through the same marshmallow. Form an X with the sticks.

2 Make two sticks that are half the length of the first ones. Use marshmallows to attach the short sticks to the top and bottom of the X.

3 Measure the height of the X. Make two sticks to match the height. Push the ends into the corner marshmallows.

4 Repeat step 1 two times. Use marshmallows to attach the new Xs together at one end. Then attach the other end of each X to one end of the first X.

5 Make four more half-size sticks. Break another stick to match the height of the X. Use them to connect the points of the Xs.

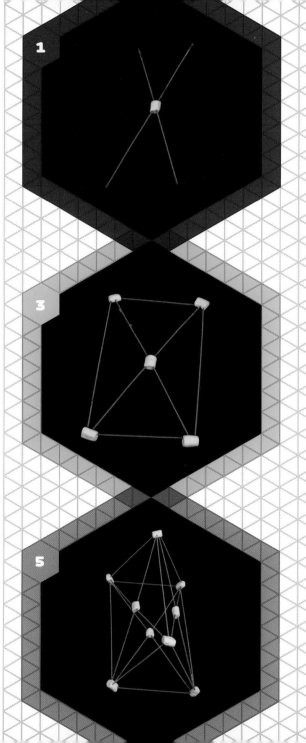

MATH TERMS

ANGLE - the shape formed when two lines meet at a common point.

DEGREE - a unit used to measure the size of an angle.

DIAGONAL - from one corner of a square or rectangle to the opposite corner.

FACE - a polygon that forms one of the flat surfaces of a 3-D shape.

HEIGHT - how tall something is.

LENGTH - the distance from one end of an object to the other.

PARALLEL - lying or moving in the same direction but always the same distance apart.

PENTAGONAL - having a five-sided shape as a base.

PRISM - a 3-D shape with parallel polygons at opposite ends and faces that are each parallelograms.

PYRAMID - a 3-D shape with triangular sides that form a point at the top.

RECTANGLE - a 2-D shape with four sides and four right angles.

SQUARE - a shape with four straight, equal sides and four equal angles.

TETRAHEDRON - a 3-D shape that has four faces.

TRIANGLE - a shape with three straight sides.

GLOSSARY

BUCKLE - to give way, bend, or collapse.

CATAPULT - an ancient military device for throwing rocks or other objects.

COMPLEX - made of many parts.

CULTURE - the ideas, traditions, art, and behaviors of a group of people.

DESTINATION - the place where you are going to.

FLING - to throw something with force.

INSERT - to stick something into something else.

MIDDLE AGES - the period of history in Europe from about AD 500 to about AD 1500.

OVERLAP - to lie partly on top of something.

SKYSCRAPER - a very tall building.

SLINGSHOT - a Y-shaped stick with an elastic band attached that is used to throw small rocks.

SPAN - to reach over or extend across something.

STACK - a pile of things placed one on top of the other.

TEMPLATE - a shape you draw or cut around to copy it onto something else.

WEB SITES

To learn more about math and science, visit ABDO Publishing Company on the World Wide Web at www.abdopublishing.com. Web sites about creative ways for kids to experience math and science are featured on our Book Links page. These links are routinely monitored and updated to provide the most current information available.

INDEX